Introduction

God told Noah to "make yourself an ark of cypress wood . . ." (Genesis 6:14). He even gave Noah very specific directions for building it. Then God told Noah just what to fill the ark with—two of each kind of animal. After Noah completed his task, God went on to perform a spectacular miracle of nature with wind, rain, and a wonderful promise of color.

This book is designed to help teachers and parents share with children the wonderful story of Noah's Ark. It is a favorite Bible story of many children as it deals with animals, weather, and the colors in the rainbow. Included in this book are ideas for presenting the Bible story and theme extensions that supplement the story. Also included are curriculum activities in art, literature, language arts, science, math, and music, as well as ideas for centers. Many patterns needed for the featured activities can be found in the book.

As you use the activities in this book, we hope that you can help the children in your care experience the many wonders involved in the story of Noah's Ark.

Ideas for Using This Book

This book provides you with wonderful ideas you can use to teach children about the story of Noah's Ark. The first several pages contain ideas for presenting the Bible story and for creating an atmosphere in your room to get the children excited about and motivated to learn about the story of Noah's Ark.

Directions for a worship area and a class mural can be found on page 2.

On page 3 are directions for making flannelboards, graphs, dice, and a diaper pin game spinner. These items will be used in many activities presented throughout the book.

A letter to parents explaining the unit on the story of Noah's Ark is found on page 4. This can be copied and sent home with each child. The letter suggests activities parents can do with their child and also asks for their help in several ways.

Pages 29–30 contain lists of children Bibles and stories you can choose from to introduce the story of Noah's Ark. Read these books to the children, help them read the books, or send them home to be read with their families. There is an endless amount of activities that can come from these books.

Ideas for Using This Book continued

Mini-units centered around the Noah's Ark story are found on pages 7–28. Each of these mini-units features a topic found in the story (animals, rain, and rainbows) and contains many fun and exciting activities relating to these topics. The activities presented involve all subject areas and include art, science, math, literature, language, music, motor skills, and even snack ideas.

Patterns for use with many of the activities throughout the book can be found on pages 31–48 and on the inside back cover.

Setting the Stage

Worship Area

Plan a special worship area where the children can gather. This area can also be used for circle time space. Use a small table to create an altar, and place a cross and a Bible on it. On the inside cover of the Bible, place a construction paper heart with the words "Jesus Loves You" written on it. When the children open the Bible, they will be reminded that it is really a story of God's love for us.

Candles are also special to have on the altar. Light the candles and sing a special song to signal to the children when you are ready to start. This encourages the children to sit quietly for the start of the Bible story of Noah's Ark. At the end of the story time, a special closing song may be sung as you blow out the candles.

Throughout the teaching of the story of Noah's Ark, place special objects on the altar to help the children remember the story of Noah's Ark. Some ideas of items to include are a small toy ark, small toy animals, and a paper rainbow.

Class Mural

Attach a large piece of roll paper to a wall. Using a marker, draw a large boat on the paper. Let the children color or paint the boat. Each day, as the children get more involved in the Noah's Ark story, have the children help you add (by drawing, painting, or even gluing on) pictures of the animals that went on Noah's Ark. Be creative. Add Noah, a ramp to the ark, a rainbow and anything else you or the children want to complete the mural. Let the children help you create a title for the mural ("God Loved Noah," "All Aboard!," etc.).

Noah's Ark

Helpful Hints

Flannelboards

Place a piece of heavy, non-fusible interfacing (available at fabric stores) over the top of a pattern page. (Patterns can be found on pages 31–48, or perhaps you have your own that you want to use.) Using a black permanent marker, trace the outline and features of the pattern. Color your pieces using erasable crayons. Cut them out. Store your flannelboard pieces in resealable plastic bags. Punch three holes in each bag and place it in a three-ring binder for easy filing and safekeeping.

Graphs

Reusable graphs can be made by drawing a grid pattern on posterboard and laminating it. Before doing a graphing activity with the children, use permanent markers to add words, pictures, and numbers. After the activity is over, the marker can be erased with fingernail polish remover. Stickers can also be used on the laminated graph. To remove stickers, use the heat from a hair dryer. The warm air softens the adhesive for easy removal.

Dice

Use one-inch (or larger) wooden cubes to make dice to fit the special needs of any activity you are doing. The dice may have numerals written on each side, all six sides having a different number, or the numbers can be repeated (having two ones, two twos, and two threes, etc.) on a die. Dotted dice can be made in the same manner as above. Words, colors, shapes, and specific numbers can also be put on dice. The possibilities are endless.

Diaper Pin Game Spinner

A simple game spinner can be made using a brad, a diaper pin, a margarine container, and a permanent marker. Many cute and colorful diaper pins are available at discount stores that may even coordinate with your game theme. Attach a diaper pin to the center of a margarine lid by punching a hole in the lid and placing a brad through the small hole at the end of the pin and then through the lid. Close the brad loosely against the back of the lid so that the pin can spin. If the pin does not spin freely, simply loosen the brad. Use a permanent marker to write any sections appropriate for the type of game you are playing on the lid. The container can be used to store the game pieces. When the lid is snapped on, the entire game can be kept in one place. The spinner may also be kept on the container while playing the game. A diaper pin can also be fastened to a laminated piece of tagboard in the same manner.

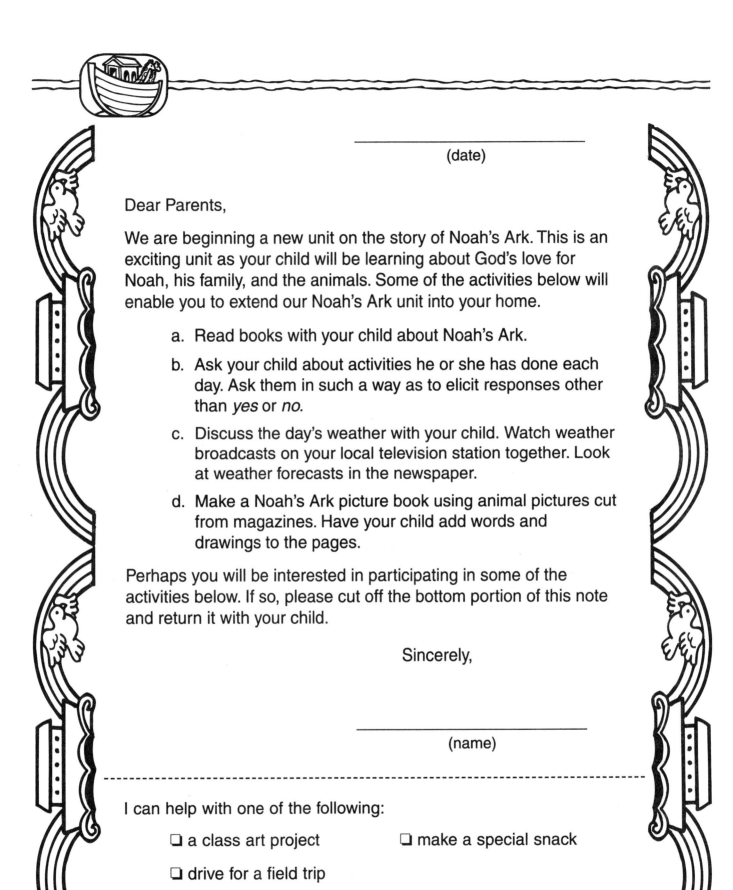

_____
(date)

Dear Parents,

We are beginning a new unit on the story of Noah's Ark. This is an exciting unit as your child will be learning about God's love for Noah, his family, and the animals. Some of the activities below will enable you to extend our Noah's Ark unit into your home.

a. Read books with your child about Noah's Ark.

b. Ask your child about activities he or she has done each day. Ask them in such a way as to elicit responses other than *yes* or *no*.

c. Discuss the day's weather with your child. Watch weather broadcasts on your local television station together. Look at weather forecasts in the newspaper.

d. Make a Noah's Ark picture book using animal pictures cut from magazines. Have your child add words and drawings to the pages.

Perhaps you will be interested in participating in some of the activities below. If so, please cut off the bottom portion of this note and return it with your child.

Sincerely,

_____
(name)

- -

I can help with one of the following:

❏ a class art project   ❏ make a special snack

❏ drive for a field trip

_____   _____
(signature)   (phone number)

Presenting the Story of Noah's Ark

Bible stories are meant to be shared. Sharing these stories using books and hands-on activities is a great way for children to have fun as they learn. The ideas below and on page 6 will help you get your children actively involved in the telling of the story.

You may wish to begin your unit on Noah's Ark (Genesis 6–9) by reading from one of the many children's Bibles available. Included on page 29 are suggestions of some Bibles and various versions of the Noah's Ark story you can choose. Before using one of the children's books to introduce the story of Noah's Ark, be sure to read through it first. Many times, major parts of the story are omitted. These children's books are good to use after you have presented the story. The children may even be able to tell you what part of the story is missing.

Tell Me a Story

Materials Needed (per child): one copy of the *Tell Me a Story* pattern page (page 31), five story markers (construction paper squares, milk jug lids, etc.)

Directions: Give each child the pattern page and five story markers. As the story of Noah's Ark is read or told, have the children place a marker over the corresponding section of the story on their page. When the story is finished, all of the pictures on the story page should be covered. Have the children take the story pages home to share the story of Noah's Ark with their families.

Noah's Ark Drama

A great way to review the story of Noah's Ark is to let the children act it out. The children can join in as each part of the story is told.

Materials Needed: pairs of tagboard copies of the mask patterns (pages 32–36), large craft sticks or paper towel tubes, glue, an imaginary ark (a large, sturdy climber works well for this), a colorful rainbow

Directions: Color the masks, laminate them, and attach them to large craft sticks or paper towel tubes. Select children to be Noah and his family (if there are not many children involved, just have Noah and his wife), and a dove. The rest of the children will be animals and will hold the masks. As you tell the story, have the children act out their part. At the end of the story, hold up the rainbow, and offer a prayer of thanks with the children.

Presenting the Story of Noah's Ark continued

Animals in the Ark

Materials Needed: a large ark shape made with tape on the floor, favorite stuffed animals (have the children bring them from home), cardboard brick building blocks

Directions: After you have introduced the story of Noah's Ark, the children will enjoy pretending to reenact it by bringing their favorite stuffed animals on the ark. Have the children build the ark using the blocks. When the ark is complete, tell the children to listen while God closes the door and the rain begins to fall. Remind them that they need to take care of their animals (feed them, brush them, and clean up after them). When the rain stops, pretend to send out the dove. Finally, tell the children that it is time to come out of the ark! Say to the children, "Wow, see the rainbow! Let's build an altar to worship and praise God." Leave the props in the room for the children to use to act out the story again during free play. The more dramatic you become with your actions and your voice, the more the children will enjoy this activity.

Noah's Ark Overlay Story

Materials Needed: copies of pattern pages 37–44 (pages 1, 3, 5, and 7 should be copied on white tagboard; pages 2, 4, 6, and 8 should be copied on overhead transparencies), loose-leaf rings, a cover page entitled "Noah's Ark"

Directions: Color the copies. (Use overhead projection markers on the transparencies.) Laminate the tagboard copies. Stack the pages face up beginning with page 1 and ending with page 8 on the

top. Then put on the cover. Attach all the copies together in this order using loose-leaf rings. To tell the story of Noah's Ark, flip the pages back to front beginning with page 1.

Variation: Make all of the copies on overhead transparencies and color them. Project the pictures onto a screen, using an overhead projector, as you tell the story. Page 2 would be placed onto the projector right over the top of page 1. Then these two pages would be removed before page 3 is put up. (Then page 4 is placed on top of page 3, page 6 on top of page 5, and page 8 on top of page 7, always removing the previous set before going on.)

Animals

God told Noah to take two of every animal into the ark. Animals are a favorite topic for young children to discuss and learn about. Below and on pages 8–15 are some great activities children can do to learn all about God's incredible creatures.

pages 8–15

— Art Ideas —

Animals in the Ark

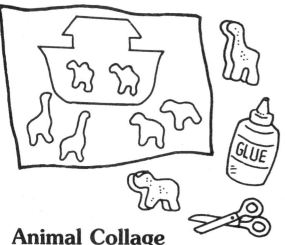

Materials Needed: one ark-shaped pattern per child (use the ark pattern on page 31; white out the words and pictures on the inside of the ark), animal-shaped sponges or cookie cutters, large sheets of paper, paint, glue

Directions: Have each child glue an ark onto a large sheet of paper. Then have the children use the cookie cutters or sponges and paint to create pairs of animals on their paper. These pictures can be displayed on a bulletin board entitled "Bring the animals two by two."

Animal Collage

Materials Needed: pictures of animals cut from newspapers, magazines, and wrapping paper; construction paper scraps; animal print fabric scraps; paintbrushes; large roll of paper; glue; scissors; small containers

Directions: Cut a large piece of paper from the roll. Set the glue out in small containers with brushes. Have the children brush on a dab of glue and then stick one of the cutout animals or pieces of fabric on the paper. The children can add any details they like using the construction paper scraps. When the project is complete, help the children add the words "Thank you, God, for animals" to the paper. This project can be completed over the course of a few days.

Animal Pairs

Materials Needed: carbon paper, white copy paper, animal stencils, pencils, paper clips

Directions: Place a piece of carbon paper between two pieces of white paper. Clip corners with paper clips. Have the children draw animals on the top sheet of white paper using the stencils. When they have finished, remove the paper clips and the carbon paper. The animals the children drew will have a matching pair on the second sheet of white paper.

Noah's Ark

Animals continued

Science Ideas

Science Table

A science table provides a wonderful way for children to touch and manipulate objects and to explore and discover. Put some of the following items out on a science table: lamb's wool, fake fur pieces, pictures of several different animal habitats and plastic toy animals for the children to place on top of the appropriate habitat pictures. (If you are working with younger children, be sure to add toy animals to your block area to encourage the children to include the Noah's Ark theme in their play.)

If you have a sand table, you may also put field corn instead of sand in the sand table for scooping, pouring, and measuring.

Field Trips

the zoo
a farm
a pet store
a hatchery

Class Pet

Let the children take care of a small animal in your room (guinea pig, rabbit, gerbil). Let families "pet sit" on weekends. Many children do not have pets at home and a classroom pet will help them understand that God's animals have needs, too (for example, food, water, a home, love).

What Do the Animals Eat?

This activity is great to do after you have presented the flannelboard activity *Feed the Animals* (page 12).

Materials Needed: tagboard copies of page 9, clear plastic report covers with slide-on plastic binders, washable markers

Directions: Color the tagboard copies and place one copy inside each plastic report cover. Hold the copy in place with the binder. Have the children take turns using the washable markers to draw lines from the animals to the food they eat. Keep a damp sponge handy to wipe off the marks the children make. As the children play this game, remind them that Noah fed the animals on the ark for God.

What Do the Animals Eat?

9

Animals continued

Animal Pairs Memory Game

Materials Needed: pairs of animal stickers, metal juice lids (from frozen concentrate), an empty plastic frosting container (to store game in)

Directions: Put one sticker on each juice lid. Have the children place the lids sticker-side down and take turns turning the lids over to find the matching pairs.

Variation: For younger children, place the lids sticker-side up and have them find the pairs. Milk jug lids or index cards can be used in place of juice can lids.

An Ark Full of Animals

Materials Needed: 9–12 half pint milk cartons with the tops cut off, scissors, a shallow box big enough to hold all the milk cartons, 9–12 small pairs of plastic toy animals, glue, cardboard ark cutout (the ark pattern on page 31 can be enlarged and used if needed)

Directions: Cut a ramp from one side of the shallow box. Glue the milk cartons to the bottom of the shallow box. Cut slits in the bottom of the cardboard ark cutout and slide it onto the back of the shallow box, over the sides. Have the children match the pairs of toy animals and place them into the rooms of the ark. Older children can practice skip counting by twos.

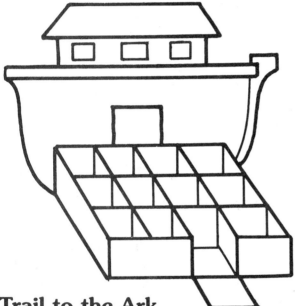

Trail to the Ark

Materials Needed: one copy of the gameboard on the inside back cover, small plastic animals, dice, crayons or markers

Directions: Color the gameboard. Mark the trail on the gameboard to begin in the grass and end at the ark.

Object: Have one child roll the die and move his or her animal the same number of spaces. The child continues rolling the die and counting off the spaces until the animal is in the ark. This game can be used individually or by small groups. (For older children, use two dice.)

Noah's Ark

Animals continued

Pairs, Pairs, Pairs

Materials Needed: pairs of some of the following items: socks, mittens, earrings, shoes, dice, buttons, etc.

Directions: Place the items on a table. Let the children sort them into pairs. As the children work, talk with them about how God had Noah bring pairs of animals into the ark.

Variation: Use many pairs of the same type of item (for example, 10 different pairs of socks).

Animal Cracker Graph

Materials Needed: 4–6 graphs (see page 3), animal crackers

Directions: Give each child a small container of animal crackers and a graph. Have the children sort their animal crackers onto the graph. What animal do they have the most of? the least of?

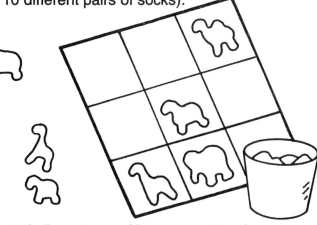

Animal Lotto

Materials Needed: animal stickers, ark pattern (page 31), five pieces of brown construction paper, a spinner (see page 3), game markers

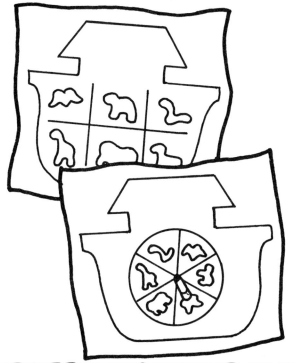

Directions: Trace the ark pattern on the five pieces of brown construction paper. To make a spinner on one of the arks you have copied, draw a large circle on the ark and divide that circle into six even sections. Place a different animal sticker in each section. Complete the spinner with a diaper pin and a brad.

On the other four arks, draw a horizontal line across the center of the ark and divide that line into thirds by drawing two vertical lines. In the six sections created on these arks, place six animal stickers that are the same pictures as the six on the spinner card. Place the stickers in a different order on each game card.

To Play: Have one child spin the spinner and place a game marker over that animal on his or her card. It is now the next child's turn. When all the children have covered all their animals, the game is over.

Animals continued

Math Ideas

Noah's Ark Dominoes

Materials Needed: animal stickers or rubber stamps, Noah's Ark stickers or rubber stamps, index cards

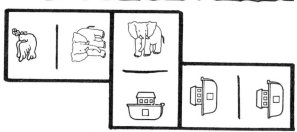

Directions: Put animal or ark stickers at opposite ends of the index cards. Some cards should have matching stickers at each end, and some cards should have different stickers at each end. Only one card should have Noah's Ark at both ends. Laminate.

To Use: Sort the cards out among the players. The player with the double Noah's Ark card begins by placing the card on the table. Players take turns matching one end of one of their cards with another card on the table.

Variation: Younger children can just lay the cards out and match up the stickers.

Literature/Language Ideas

Feed the Animals

Materials Needed: flannelboard figures (use the animal patterns from page 9 and the patterns on page 47; see page 3 for directions on making flannelboard pieces), a flannelboard

Directions: Place the flannelboard pieces on the flannelboard as you tell the story below.

Noah and his wife got up early one morning to feed the animals. (Place the figures of Noah, his wife, and the animals on the board.) They fed the elephants some fish, the bears some leaves, the monkeys some grass, the frogs some fruit, the giraffes some vegetables, and the rabbits some flies. (Place these foods next to each animal.) When they were done, they went off to have their own breakfast. As they sat down to eat, they heard the animals making terrible noises. They went to see what was happening. Do you know why the animals were so unhappy? Help Noah and his wife give the right food to the animals.

Hint: Bears eat fish; elephants eat grass; monkeys eat fruit; giraffes eat leaves; frogs eat flies; and rabbits eat vegetables. Have the children place the foods next to the animals that eat them. Older children could make pictures of a simple life cycle (for example, man eats cow; cow eats grass.).

Noah's Creative Writing

Materials Needed: white paper, Noah's Ark rubber stamp

Directions: Stamp Noah's Ark on each piece of paper. Have each child write or dictate a story about Noah's Ark. Each child could choose an animal and write how Noah took care of it on the ark. Or, you could have the children draw a storm scene and write about the storm that God sent.

Animals continued

— Literature/Language Ideas —

Noah's Ark Big Book

Materials Needed: an ark-shaped book page per child (pattern page 31), ark-shaped front and back covers, animal sponges, paint, cookie cutters, crayons or markers, loose-leaf rings, stencils or rubber stamps (optional)

Directions: Give each child a book page. Have the children make a pair of one kind of animal on the page. They may draw, sponge paint, or stamp the animals on the paper. Then have each child complete the following sentence on the paper: "There were two _____ on Noah's Ark." (Older children may write their own sentence.) Laminate the finished pages along with the front and back covers. Attach the pages with loose-leaf rings.

There were two lions on Noah's ark.

— Music/Large Motor Ideas —

Sail Away
(Tune: "Muffin Man")

Oh, Noah built the ark for God,
The ark for God, the ark for God.
Oh, Noah built the ark for God
And then they sailed away!

Oh, the animals came on two by two,
Two by two, two by two.
The animals came on two by two,
And then they sailed away!

It rained and poured for forty days,
Forty days, forty days.
It rained and poured for forty days,
And then they sailed away!

The sun came out and dried the land,
Dried the land, dried the land.
The sun came out and dried the land.
Now they won't sail away!

The rainbow filled the sunny sky,
The sunny sky, the sunny sky.
The rainbow filled the sunny sky,
And they thanked God that day!

Two By Two
(Tune: "This Old Man")

verse 1 Two by two, two by two
The animals came on two by two.
There were slithering snakes
And jumping kangaroos
They filled the ark up
Two by two.

verse 2 Two by two, two by two
The animals came on two by two.
There were pigs that oinked
And cows that mooed.
They filled the ark up
Two by two.

verse 3 There were lions, tigers,
And bears, too.

verse 4 There were frogs that jumped
And doves that cooed.

verse 5 There was almost no room
For Noah and his crew.

Let the children help you make up other verses.

Animals continued

Feeding Time

Materials Needed: flannelboard pieces (pages 45–47) made using the directions given on page 3, a triangle rhythm instrument, a copy of the "Feeding Time" chant below

Directions: Place the pieces on the flannelboard as you introduce the "Feeding Time" chant to the children using a steady beat. Divide the children into five groups and have each group make the sound for one verse. Each group of children should begin its sound at the point in the chant where it is introduced and keep making that sound throughout the rest of the chant. Ring the triangle for the dinner bell. When you reach the last verse, all of the groups should be making their sound. Let this continue for a few minutes. It is fun to record this on a tape and let the children listen to themselves. This chant can also be sung to the tune of "Six Little Ducks."

Feeding Time

It was feeding time on the floating zoo.
The cows in their stall were beginning to moo.

MOO!   MOO!   MOO!   MOO!

The lions and tigers—in all there were four—
Were so impatient, they began to roar.

ROAR!   ROAR!   ROAR!   ROAR!

The gorillas and monkeys were hungry, too!
They made it known with their loud oo-oo!

OO-OO!   OO-OO!   OO-OO!   OO-OO!

In all this noise, the ark still sat
In a pouring rain that went pit-pat.

PIT-PAT!   PIT-PAT!   PIT-PAT!   PIT-PAT!

Poor Noah around the ark did rush.
He said, "No dinner, if you don't HUSH!"

SH!   SH!   SH!   SH!

And then they all heard the dinner bell chime.
All over the ark, it was feeding time!

DING DONG!   DING DONG!
MOO! MOO! MOO! MOO!
ROAR! ROAR! ROAR! ROAR!
OO-OO! OO-OO! OO-OO! OO-OO!
PIT-PAT! PIT-PAT! PIT-PAT! PIT-PAT!
SH! SH! SH! SH!
SLURP! SLURP! SLURP! SLURP!
MMMM DELICIOUS!

Noah's Ark

Animals continued

Animal Movement Cards

Materials Needed: pictures of animals mounted on different colors of tagboard and labeled with a written phrase about how the animal moves (crawl like a turtle, hop like a frog, etc.); Laminate the cards for durability.

Directions: Have a child select one of the cards. Have (or help) the child read it. All the children begin to move like that animal. Repeat this using the other cards for as long as the activity holds the children's interest. This activity may also be used when you teach the story of creation.

More Songs

There are many songs about Noah's Ark available. Check your local Christian bookstore.

— Snack Idea —

Ark Snack

Materials Needed: graham cracker squares, peanut butter or frosting, animal crackers, plastic knives

Directions: Have the children spread frosting or peanut butter on graham cracker squares. Then have them find pairs of animal crackers and stand them on the top of each square. Let the children eat and enjoy! This snack may also be enjoyed when the story of Daniel in the Lions' Den (Daniel 6) is taught by using only lion crackers.

— Another Idea —

Other Bible Stories

Creation (Genesis 1)
Daniel in the Lions' Den (Daniel 6)

Noah's Ark

Rain

When Noah and his family, along with all the animals, were safely inside the ark, the rain began to fall. It rained for 40 days and nights. A unit on rain can be the introduction to a whole year of activities on the seasonal weather changes which occur in your area of the country.

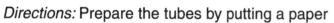

— Art Ideas —

Rainsticks

Real rainsticks can be purchased at nature stores. You may wish to have one available to show the children before beginning this project.

Materials Needed: one toilet paper or paper towel tube per child, two white paper baking cups per child (to fit over the end of the tube), brown tissue paper (cut into small squares), rice or popcorn kernels, masking tape, glue, paintbrushes

Directions: Prepare the tubes by putting a paper baking cup over one end of each tube and taping it securely with masking tape. Have each child put about one tablespoon of popcorn kernels or rice in the tube. Close off the other end of the tube using a paper baking cup and tape. Then have each child brush glue over the outside of the tube and stick the brown tissue paper squares on. Encourage the children to cover their tube completely. Let them dry. Have the children shake them and listen to the rain! Rainsticks could also be made and/or used with the story of Jesus calming the storm (Matthew 8, Mark 4, Luke 8). Older children could make up songs about rain and shake their rainsticks as they sing them.

Raindrop Paintings

Materials Needed: plastic bubble wrap (the kind that is used to wrap packages), large sheets of white paper, blue paint, paintbrushes, tape

Directions: Tape the bubble wrap to a tabletop. Have the children take turns using the brushes to paint on the bubble wrap. When each child has finished his or her area, lay a piece of white paper over the area to make a print of it. The next child can paint right over the same area.

Note: When dry, let the children add cutouts of Noah's Ark to their paper.

Variation: Cover the entire tabletop with bubble wrap. After the children have painted the whole piece of bubble wrap, lay a piece of bulletin board paper on the top and make a print of it. When dry, use this to cover a bulletin board. Have the children write or dictate an experience about rainy/stormy weather on raindrop-shaped paper. Display these on the bulletin board with the caption "I am with you always" (Matthew 28:20).

Rain continued

— Art Ideas —

Rain Clouds

Materials Needed: large paper plates (cut in half); yarn, crêpe paper, or iridescent wrapping paper cut in ¼" strips (blue, gray, and white are good colors); gray paint; sponges; cotton balls; glue

Directions: Have each child sponge paint one side of a paper plate half using gray paint. Let dry. Next, have the children glue crêpe paper streamers, yarn, or wrapping paper along the bottom edge for rain. Then have them glue cotton balls along the cut edge of the plate.

Variations: Help the children write "Thank You, God, for Rain" on the plates and hang them from the ceiling. To display them on a bulletin board, add the words written above on a cloud-shaped piece of paper and attach it as a title. Older children could list or make collages of all the things for which water is good.

Cloud Paintings

Materials Needed: white or gray fingerpaint (gray can be made by adding a little black paint to the white paint), plastic cafeteria trays, white or light blue construction paper

Directions: Have each child fingerpaint on a tray using his or her choice of paint color. When finished, have the children place their paper on the tray and make a cloud print by laying the paper on the paint and rubbing their hands over the paper.

Note: This can be also be done right on a plastic-topped table. The paint washes off easily.

Variation: These pages can also be compiled to make a group book. Have the children write or dictate stories about rain. Title the book "God Gives Us Rain."

Umbrella Art

Materials Needed: umbrella shapes cut from manila paper, colored tissue paper scraps, spray bottles, water, colored construction paper, easels, glue, scissors

Directions: Help each child hang an umbrella shape on an easel. Have the children take turns lightly spraying their paper with water using the spray bottle. Next, have them stick the pieces of colored tissue paper to their paper. Then have them lightly spray their paper again. Take the umbrella off of the easel and lay the paper flat to dry. When dry, the pieces of tissue paper will lift off the paper, leaving pretty colored designs. Show the children how to attach a handle cut from colored construction paper to each umbrella.

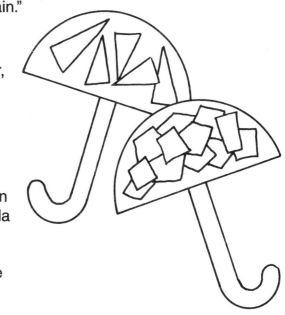

Rain continued

Science Table

Place the items below on a science table for the children to manipulate and observe.

Tornado Bottle—Tornado Tubes™ can be purchased at school supply or nature stores. Attach a Tornado Tube™ to two plastic soda pop bottles to make a tornado bottle.

rain water—Collect some in a white dish and let the children look at it with a magnifying glass to determine if it is clean or not.

photographs of storms

Teakettle Rain

Materials Needed: a teakettle, water, aluminum pie pan, ice cubes

Directions: Bring the water in the teakettle to a boil so that steam is rising out of the spout. Put the ice cubes in the pie pan and hold it over the spout of the teakettle so that the steam hits the bottom of the pan. The steam will cool and condense forming droplets on the outside of the pan. The droplets will collect and fall like rain falling from a cloud. See if any older children can tell you about the water cycle or draw a picture of it.

Caution: This activity should be done by adults and observed by children.

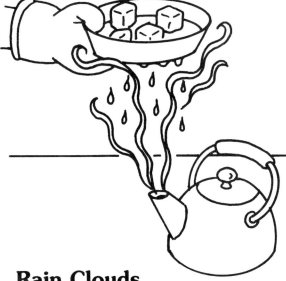

Rain Clouds

God gave us ways to anticipate changes in the weather. Brainstorm with the children about ways we can tell when it is going to rain (the changes in the clouds, the wind, etc.). Then try the activity below.

Materials Needed: cobalt chloride (see if you can get some from a school science teacher), coffee filter, white construction paper

Directions: Soak the coffee filter with cobalt chloride and let it dry. Cut a cloud shape out of the white paper and attach the dry coffee filter to it. (These steps should be done by an adult.) The cloud will tell the children when it is going to rain. The paper on the cloud changes color when there is more moisture in the air. Misting lightly with water will also cause the paper to change color.

Rain continued

God's Weather Days

Rain isn't the only type of weather God gives us. With the children, make a list of other kinds of weather and then introduce this activity.

Materials Needed: a blank calendar page with 2" x 2" squares, tagboard copies of the weather squares (page 47)

Directions: Each day for one month, have the children decide what the predominant weather of the day is (cloudy, snowy, rainy, etc.). Let them take turns placing the corresponding weather square on the calendar space for that day. At the end of the month, help the children use the weather squares to graph the results on the *God's Weather Days Graph*. (See directions below.)

WEATHER TRACKER

God's Weather Days Graph

Use this activity after using the *God's Weather Days* activity above.

Materials Needed: a graph (see page 3), copies of the weather squares (page 47)

Directions: Using the graph, have the children help you place some of the weather squares in the grid. Compare the results. Ask the children what kind of weather (rainy, snowy, etc.) there was the most of and the least of.

Umbrella File Folder Game

Materials Needed: 6–8 umbrella shapes in a variety of sizes cut from wallpaper, tagboard, a file folder, black construction paper, glue, scissors

Directions: Glue the umbrella cutouts to the tagboard. Laminate them and cut them out. Trace the umbrellas on the black construction paper and cut them out. Glue the black umbrella cutouts to the file folder. Laminate.

To Use: Have the children take turns matching the wallpaper umbrellas to the matching black umbrella shadows. (This activity promotes visual discrimination.) Older children can cut out an umbrella from wallpaper, glue it to a sheet of paper, and write a poem about rain to the left and right of the handle.

Rain continued

Weather Patterns

Materials Needed: weather rubber stamps or weather stickers; long, narrow strips of paper

Directions: Begin a pattern on the narrow strips of paper using either the weather rubber stamps or stickers. Have children take turns finishing the pattern.

Variation: After the children have experienced this activity, have them use the stamps or stickers to create their own patterns. They can also put the stamps/stickers on paper to create a story about weather. On each child's sheet of paper, write "God gave us ___." Have the children stamp a weather symbol on the blank space and then complete the sentence.

— Literature/Language Idea —

Spilt Milk Big Book

Sometimes it looked like __a flower__, but it wasn't __a flower__.

This activity is perfect to use after reading the book *It Looked Like Spilt Milk*, by Charles G. Shaw (HarperCollins, 1988).

Materials Needed: blue and white construction paper, glue, a front and back cover, loose-leaf rings

Directions: Have (or help) each child write "Sometimes it looked like _____, but it wasn't _____." on the bottom of a sheet of blue construction paper. Then have each child tear a shape out of a piece of white construction paper and glue it to the top of the blue construction paper. Help the child fill in the blanks on the bottom of the page. Put the title "It Looked Like Spilt Milk" on the front cover. Laminate the covers and the pages. Put the book together with loose-leaf rings.

— Music/Large Motor Ideas —

Rain, Rain Go Away
(Tune: same)

Rain, rain, go away.
Come again another day.
We need some sunshine on this day
So we can all go out and play.

Rain, rain, must you pour?
Noah just can't take much more.
Rain so wet and clouds so dark—
It's just too crowded on this ark!

Rain, rain, please stop now.
Noah's got a cranky cow.
Please, sun, can't you shine?
He hates to hear her cry and whine.

"Rain, rain, I beg of you!"
Noah says. He's grouchy, too.
Rain sloushes, beats, and pours
While sheep bleat and lions roar.

Dear God, what do I see?
Is that rainbow just for me?
Rain, rain, yes, go away,
So Noah's friends can go and play.

Rain continued

Build, Build, Build the Ark
(Tune: "Row, Row, Row Your Boat")

Build, build, build the ark.
Time is growing short.
Gather animals two by two,
That buzz and grunt and snort.

Rain, rain, and rain some more
For forty days and nights.
Covering all the valleys and hills
'Til no more land's in sight.

Sail, sail, sail the ark
On the water blue
Noisily, noisily, noisily, noisily
In Noah's floating zoo.

Rain Sounds in God's World
The children can use the movements described
below to create a rainstorm right in the classroom.

Rub fingers together for raindrops.
Rub hands together for a gentle rain.
Pat thighs for the rainstorm.
Reverse the order to end the rainstorm.

Use these rain sounds in God's world with the story of
Jesus calming the storm (Matthew 8, Mark 4, Luke 8).

The Itsy-Bitsy Spider
(Tune: same)

The itsy-bitsy spider went up the water spout.
Down came the rain and washed the spider out.
Out came the sun and dried up all the rain
And the itsy-bitsy spider went up the spout again.

The itsy-bitsy spider went up the water spout.
The rain came again and washed the spider out.
Noah came along and said, "Better come with me,
Before this water spout is underneath the sea."

The itsy-bitsy spider found the ark was watertight.
With his spider wife for forty days and nights.
Out came the sun and dried up all the rain
And out of the ark the itsy-bitsy spiders came.

Rainy Weather
(Tune: "Blue Bird")

Rainy weather, stormy weather
   (Circle around for first three lines.)
Rainy weather, stormy weather
When the wind blows,
We all come together.
   (Come together in center.)
Three steps back and 1, 2, 3!
   (Spoken and step back.)

He's Got the Whole World in His Ark
(Tune: same)

He's got stamping horses in his ark.
He's got stamping horses in his ark.
He's got stamping horses in his ark.
He's got the whole world in his ark.

2. waddling ducks
3. flapping flamingos
4. hopping bullfrogs
5. swinging monkeys
6. crawling crocodiles
7. running children
8. sleeping kittens

Other Bible Stories About Rain or Storms
Jesus Calming the Storm (Matthew 8, Mark 4, Luke 8)
Jonah and the Whale (Jonah 1 and 2)
Elijah and the Rain (1 Kings 17 and 18)

Rainbows

God placed a rainbow in the sky as his promise that he would never again send a flood to destroy Earth and as a reminder of his love for all living creatures. A unit on rainbows can very easily include activities on colors. Once you have introduced this mini-unit, extend it by having special color days.

Art Ideas

Rainbow Collage

Materials Needed: large white bulletin board paper, scraps of construction paper in rainbow colors, rainbow-colored items cut from magazines, glue, paintbrushes, markers, scissors

Directions: Using the markers, draw a large rainbow arc on the paper and cut it out. Lightly color in each of the sections so that the children will know which color goes in each section. Have the children brush glue in each section and cover it with magazine pictures and scraps of the appropriate color. Label it with the heading "God Keeps His Promises!" This is a good group activity which can be worked on over a period of days.

Paper Plate Noah's Ark

Materials Needed: two paper plates and one brad per child, markers or crayons, brown paint and paintbrushes, animal crackers

Directions: Cut one paper plate in half and staple the two pieces together along the rounded edge. Then have the children paint a brown ark on the plate.

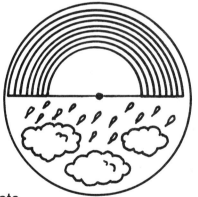

Draw a line across the whole diameter of the second plate. Have the children use markers or crayons to make raindrops and clouds on the top half of the plate. Then turn the plate so that the blank half becomes the top and have the children draw a rainbow. (The raindrops will be upside down as the children draw the rainbow.)

Attach the brown ark plate to the raindrop/rainbow plate using a brad by lining up the rounded edges of the two paper plates. Let the children put some animal crackers in their ark. When the large plate is turned, the ark will be in the rain and then under the rainbow.

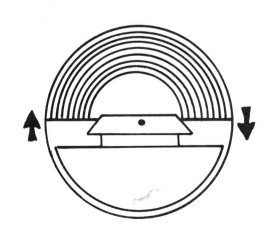

Rainbows continued

Shapes Rainbow

Materials Needed: a rainbow outlined on a large roll of paper; sponges cut in seven different shapes (triangle, circle, etc.); red, orange, yellow, green, blue, indigo, and violet paint

Directions: Have the children work together to create a rainbow. For each color of the rainbow, have the children use a different shape of sponge to paint the predrawn arc. Add big, white cloud cutouts at each end of the arc and the following words in them: "I have set my rainbow in the clouds . . ." (Genesis 9:13).

I have set my rainbow in the clouds.

Rainbow Paint

Materials Needed: a small can of evaporated milk, food coloring, plastic foam egg carton (remove top and cut bottom part in half so that you have two six-egg sections), cotton swabs, white paper, tablespoon

Directions: Put about one tablespoon of evaporated milk in each egg carton section. Add food coloring and mix to make the desired colors (the more food coloring, the brighter the colors). Using cotton swabs, have the children paint with these rainbow paints on the white paper. When this paint dries, it will be shiny.

Variation: Cut the paper in the shape of a piece of bread. Display the finished paintings on a wall or a bulletin board and add the words "Give Us Today Our Daily Bread" (Matthew 6:11). Older children can make a menu for a lunch or dinner including foods from all of the food groups.

Note: This activity can be done with the *Rainbow Toast* activity on page 28.

Science Table

Display the objects listed below on your science table so the children can experiment with color and light.

prisms
kaleidoscopes
rainbow glasses—available in nature stores
color paddles
crystals—Hang them above a table or in windows.

Rainbows

On a warm, sunny day, attach a nozzle to a hose that will provide a fine mist of water to make rainbows. Remember to watch for rainbows naturally occurring after rain.

Rainbows continued

— Science Ideas —

Colorful Flowers

Discuss with the children how God created living things to need water. Ask the children the question, "How do you think plants get their water?" Then complete the experiment below.

Materials Needed: clear containers of water (plastic peanut butter jars work well), food coloring, white flowers—carnations or Queen Anne's lace—and/or celery stalks

Directions: Add food coloring to the water in the containers. Put the flowers or celery stalks into the jars. As the flower or celery takes in water, it will begin to turn the same color as the water in the jar.

Color Mixing

Materials Needed: food coloring; six small, clear containers (medicine cups work well); water; eyedroppers; tray

Directions: Fill three containers with water and tint each one a different primary color (red, blue, yellow). Put these on a tray along with three more containers of water. Have a child use the eyedroppers to add drops of colored water to the clear containers. What happens when they put two different colors into a container?

Variation: After they have mixed the colors, have the children use the eyedroppers to drip their new colors onto coffee filters.

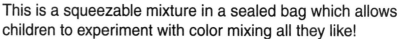

Rainbow Bag

This is a squeezable mixture in a sealed bag which allows children to experiment with color mixing all they like!

Materials Needed: For each batch—a medium saucepan, ⅓ cup of sugar, 1 cup of cornstarch, 4 cups of cold water, food coloring, resealable sandwich bags, 3 bowls, spoons, tablespoon

Directions: Mix sugar, cornstarch, and cold water in the saucepan. Heat until it begins to thicken, stirring constantly. Cool. Divide the mixture equally into three bowls. Then add one color (blue, red, yellow) of food coloring to each bowl, stirring until the desired color is reached. Put a heaping tablespoonful of each color of mixture into a resealable sandwich bag and seal. Children can squish the bag with their hands mixing the colors. Refrigerate any unused mixture.

Rainbows continued

Favorite Color Graph

Materials Needed: a graph (see page 3) labeled with children's favorite colors, stickers or construction paper squares that correspond to the colors on the graph

Directions: Have each child choose a sticker to represent his or her favorite color and write his or her name on it. Then stick it to the graph in the row which corresponds with child's chosen color.

Compare and discuss the results.

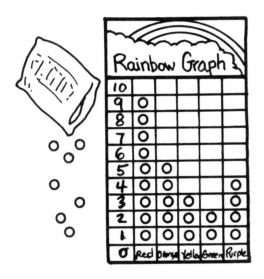

Rainbow Candy Graph

Materials Needed: four tagboard copies of a graph (see page 3), one snack-size bag of candy that comes in a variety of colors (for example, M&Ms™ or Skittles™), snack-size resealable bags

Directions: Color the tagboard copies of the graphs to correspond with the colors of candies in the snack-size bags. Laminate them. Working with four children at a time, give each child a bag of candy and have him or her fill in the graph. Which color do they have the most of? the least of? Do they have the same amount of a certain color? Who has the most of a certain color? When they have completed the activity, let the children eat a few of their candies and put the rest in their resealable snack bag. Send the candy home with a note explaining the activity.

Rainbow Sorting

Materials Needed: a piece of tagboard, plastic milk jug lids or old magic marker caps in rainbow colors, crayons or markers

Directions: Draw and color a large rainbow on the piece of tagboard and laminate it. Have the children sort the milk lids or marker caps onto the corresponding color arc of the rainbow.

Variation: Older children may count the total number of lids of each color and compare the number. Two or more colors can be grouped together to make an addition sentence.

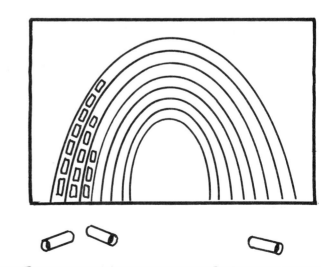

Rainbows continued

Literature/Language Ideas

Color Bags

Introduce this activity with the book *Of Colors and Things*, by Tana Hoban (Greenwillow, 1989).

Materials Needed: a variety of colors of paper craft bags (available in school supply stores), similar colors of construction paper

Directions: Divide the children into small groups. Give each group a different-colored bag. Have the children look around the room and collect in their bag objects that are the same color as the bag. Then get back together as a whole group and let each small group show the items that it found. Display the items on pieces of like-colored construction paper on a table or a shelf for a few days.

As a follow-up activity, have the children think about things God created. They can then draw pictures of or list things in nature that are the same color as the bag they used.

All Day Long Big Book

Introduce this activity by reading the book *Mary Wore Her Red Dress and Henry Wore His Green Sneakers* by Merle Peek (Houghton Mifflin, 1993).

Materials Needed: a photograph of each child, colored construction-paper copies of page 48, front and back covers, loose-leaf rings

Directions: Glue each child's photograph onto a book page. Have the children fill in the blanks with a phrase describing one of the items of clothing that they are wearing in the photograph. Make a title page and laminate all the pages. Bind the pages together using the loose-leaf rings.

Music/Large Motor Ideas

Rainbow Streamers Dance

Materials Needed: crêpe paper streamers in rainbow colors, a recording of the song "Rainbow Connection" from *The Muppet Movie* or "Somewhere Over the Rainbow" from *The Wizard of Oz* movie

Directions: Have the children dance and wave the streamers as the music plays. Encourage them to experiment with the streamers by waving them high and low or by twirling them. What other movements can they think of? Children can also dance and wave the streamers while singing the song *Rainy Weather* (page 21).

Rainbows continued

Rainbow Exchange

Materials Needed: enough 2" x 6" strips of tagboard (red, orange, yellow, green, blue, indigo, and violet) for each child to use one (laminated for durability)

Directions: Have the children form a circle. Give each child one colored strip, alternating the colors around the circle. When you call out a color, the children holding that color exchange places within the circle. When you call out "Rainbow Exchange," all the children change places.

The More we get together

Rainbow Prayer
(Tune: "We Gather Together")

We gather together as part of God's rainbow,
As brothers and sisters from all 'round the world.
With patience and caring, his blessings we are sharing.
Sing praises to his name; he made us his own.

We gather together as part of God's rainbow,
A rainbow of people who color God's world.
In all situations, we are still divine creations.
Sing praises to his name; he made us his own.

We gather together as part of God's rainbow,
With animals, plants, and the whole of the Earth.
As part of his colors, we must care for all the others.
Sing praises to his name; he made us his own.

Who Is Wearing Something Blue?
(Tune: "London Bridge")

Who is wearing something blue,
Something blue, something blue,
If you're wearing something blue,
Tap your shoes.

Repeat using the following colors:
Who is wearing something red—Tap your head.
Who is wearing something yellow—Shake like a bowl of Jell-O™.
Who is wearing something green—Jump like a jumping bean.
Who is wearing something brown—Turn around and 'round.
Who is wearing something black—Pat yourself on the back.
Who is wearing something pink—Both eyes quickly blink.
Who is wearing something white—Twist with all your might.
Who is wearing something gray—Your arms should swing and sway.
Who is wearing orange clothes—Tap your nose.
Who is wearing something purple—Drink some purple slurple.

Red, Yellow, Blue, I Love You
(Tune: "Three Blind Mice")

Red, yellow, blue,
I love you.
Red, yellow, blue,
Yes, it's true.
You are the primary colors.
You can make all the others,
Like colorful sisters and
    brothers.
I love you,
Red, yellow, blue.

Orange, purple, green,
A delight to be seen.
Orange, purple, green,
Like pumpkins, grapes, and
    beans.
Secondary colors you are.
But still you are colorful
    stars,
In rainbows, flowers, and
    houses, and cars,
A delight to be seen,
Orange, purple, green.

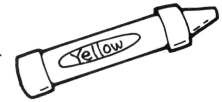

Rainbows continued

Just as Noah gave thanks to God for keeping his family safe during the flood, we too can offer thanks to God for providing us with a snack each day.

Rainbow Toast

Materials Needed: milk, food coloring, small plastic cups, cotton swabs, white bread, toaster(s), tablespoon

Directions: Put about one tablespoon of milk in each plastic cup. Add food coloring and mix to make seven different colors. Have the children use the cotton swabs to paint designs with the colored milk on their slice of bread. Toast and enjoy! It's amazing, but Rainbow Toast is best eaten without butter!

Note: If you use this activity along with the *Rainbow Paint* activity (page 23), you can use the remainder of the can of evaporated milk in place of regular milk.

Rainbow Kabobs

Materials Needed: wooden skewers, fruit pieces (strawberries, cantaloupe, watermelon, blueberries, honeydew, apples, grapes, etc.)

Directions: Have the children make a rainbow kabob for a snack by alternating different colored pieces of fruit on their skewer. As the children snack on their rainbow kabobs, talk with them about other colorful food God has made (corn, broccoli, eggplant, etc.).

Rainbow Cookies

Materials Needed: one package of refrigerated sugar cookie dough, food coloring

Directions: Open the cookie dough and divide it into four sections. Add food coloring to make one section each of red, yellow, blue, and green dough. Roll each color of dough into a ten-inch snake. Slightly flatten the green, yellow, and red rolls. Layer the flattened rolls on top of the blue roll in this order—green, yellow, and red. You should have a rainbow arc.
Wrap in plastic wrap and refrigerate until ready to use.

To Use: Cut roll into ¼-inch slices and bake according to package directions.

   Noah's Ark

Book References

Children's Bibles

The Beginner's Bible: Timeless Children's Stories by Karyn Henley (Questar, 1989)

Read Aloud Bible Stories Vol. 3 by Ella K. Lindvall (Moody Press, 1990)

The Tiny Tots Bible Story Book by John Walton and Kim Walton (David C. Cook, 1993)

Toddlers Bedtime Storybook by V. Gilbert Beers (Victor, 1992)

The Toddler's Bible by V. Gilbert Beers (Victor, 1992)

Tomie De Paola's Book of Bible Stories by Tomie De Paola (Putnam, 1990)

Noah's Ark Stories

The Ark by Arthur Geisert (Houghton Mifflin, 1988)

Drip Drop by Mary Manz Simon (Concordia, 1990)

Noah and the Ark and the Animals by Andrew Clements (Scholastic, 1992)

Noah's Ark by Lucy Cousins (Candlewick Press, 1993)

Noah's Ark by Linda Hayward (Random House, 1987)

Noah's Ark by Lawrence T. Lorimer (Random House, 1978)

Noah's Ark by Peter Spier (Dell, 1992)

Old Noah's Elephants by Warren Ludwig (Putnam, 1991)

One Wide River to Cross adapted by Barbara Emberley (Little, 1992)

Por Que Noe Eligio la Paloma: Why Noah Chose the Dove by Isaac Bashevis Singer (Farrar, Straus & Giroux, 1992)

Two by Two by Barbara Reid (Scholastic, 1993)

Animal Stories

Aardvarks, Disembark! by Ann Jonas (Puffin, 1994)

All God's Critters Got a Place in the Choir by Bill Staines (Puffin, 1993)

Animals in Hiding by Melvin Berger (Newbridge Communications, 1993)

Hey! Get Off Our Train by John Burningham (Crown Books, 1994)

Look! The Ultimate Spot-the-Difference Book by A.J. Wood (Puffin, 1993)

What Comes in Twos, Threes & Fours? by Suzanne Aker (Simon & Schuster, 1992)

Where Do Animals Live? by Melvin Berger (Newbridge Communications, 1994)

 **Book References continued**

Rain Stories

Amy Loves the Rain by Julia Hoban (HarperCollins, 1993)

The Cloud's Journey by Sigrid Heuck (Atomium Books, 1991)

Cloudy With a Chance of Meatballs by Judi Barrett (Macmillan, 1982)

It Looked Like Spilt Milk by Charles G. Shaw (HarperCollins, 1988)

It's Raining, It's Pouring by Kim Eagle (Whispering Coyote Press, 1994)

The Itsy Bitsy Spider retold and illustrated by Iza Trapani (Whispering Coyote Press, 1993)

Just a Thunderstorm by Gina Mayer and Mercer Mayer (Western, 1993)

Listen to the Rain by Bill Martin, Jr. and John Archambault (Henry Holt, 1988)

Peter Spier's Rain by Peter Spier (Doubleday, 1987)

Rain by Robert Kalan (Morrow, 1991)

Rain by Rozanne Williams (Creative Teaching Press, 1994)

Rain Talk by Mary Serfozo (MacMillan, 1990)

Umbrella by Taro Yashima (Puffin, 1977)

Weather Words and What They Mean by Gail Gibbons (Holiday, 1989)

Wet World by Norma Simon (Candlewick Press, 1995)

Who Cares About the Weather? by Melvin Berger (Newbridge Communications, 1992)

Rainbow Stories

Brown Bear, Brown Bear, What Do You See? by Bill Martin, Jr. (Henry Holt, 1983)

Color Dance by Ann Jonas (Greenwillow, 1989)

Color Farm by Lois Ehlert (HarperCollins, 1990)

Color Zoo by Lois Ehlert (HarperCollins, 1989)

Is It Red? Is It Yellow? Is It Blue? by Tana Hoban (Morrow, 1987)

Little Blue and Little Yellow by Leo Lionni (Morrow, 1994)

Mary Wore Her Red Dress and Henry Wore His Green Sneakers by Merle Peek (Houghton Mifflin, 1993)

The Mixed-Up Chameleon by Eric Carle (HarperCollins, 1988)

Mouse Paint by Ellen Stoll Walsh (Harcourt Brace Jovanovich, 1991)

Of Colors and Things by Tana Hoban (Greenwillow, 1989)

Planting a Rainbow by Lois Ehlert (Harcourt Brace Jovanovich, 1988)

The Rainbow Fish by Marcus Pfister (North-South Books, 1992)

A Rainbow of My Own by Don Freeman (Viking Child Books, 1966)

Red Day, Green Day by Edith Kunhardt (Greenwillow, 1992)

For use with *Tell Me a Story* (page 5), *Animals in the Ark* (page 7), *An Ark Full of Animals* (page 10), *Animal Lotto* (page 11), and *Noah's Ark Big Book* (page 13)

Noah's Ark

For use with *Noah's Ark Drama* (page 5)

Noah's Ark

For use with *Noah's Ark Drama* (page 5)

For use with *Noah's Ark Drama* (page 5)

For use with *Noah's Ark Drama* (page 5)

For use with *Noah's Ark Drama* (page 5)

36

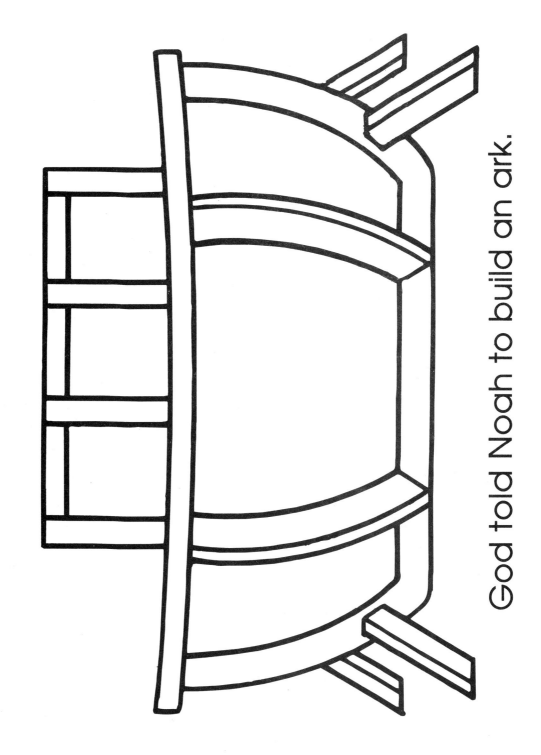

God told Noah to build an ark.

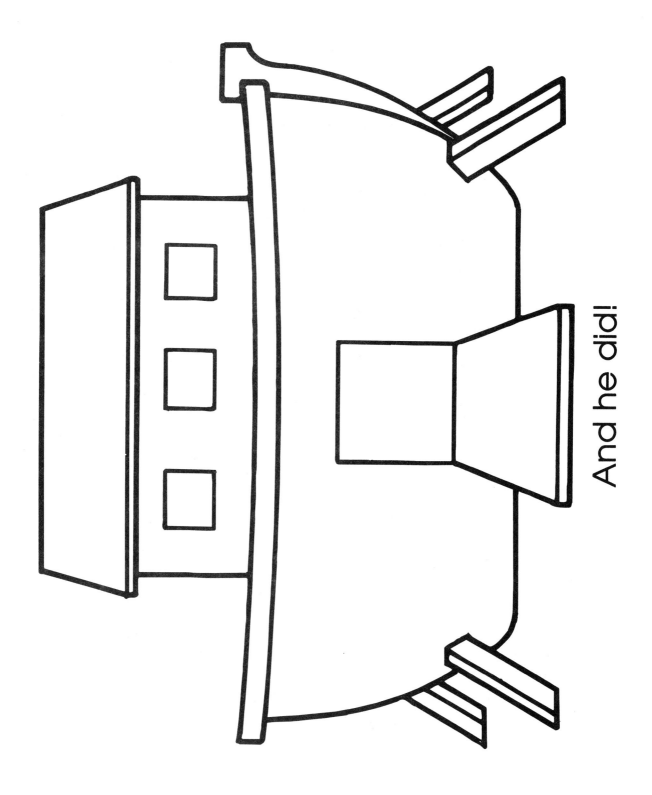

And he did!

God told Noah to take two of every kind of animal on the ark.

And he did!

God told Noah he was going to send a flood.

And he did!

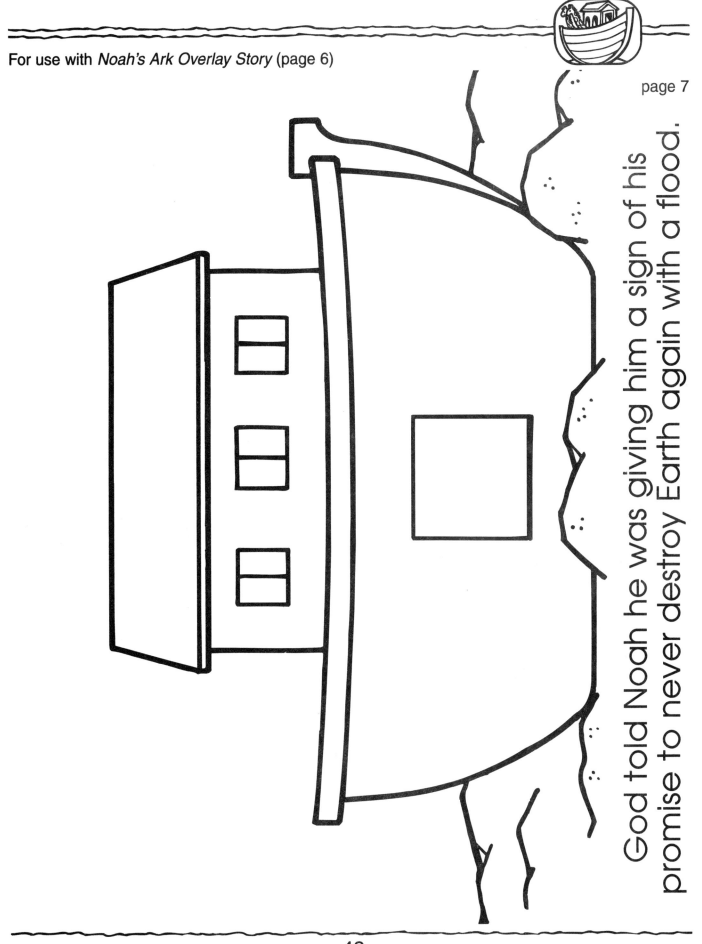

God told Noah he was giving him a sign of his promise to never destroy Earth again with a flood.

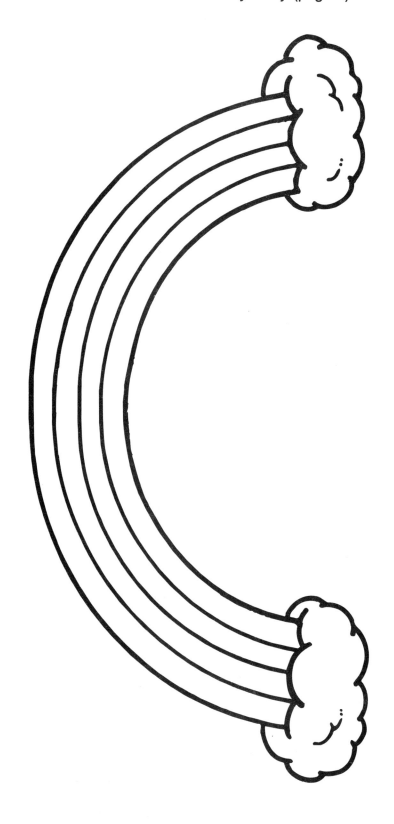

And he did!

For use with *Feeding Time* (page 14)

45

For use with *Feeding Time* (page 14)

Noah's Ark

Noah and his wife patterns for use with *Feed the Animals* (page 12) and *Feeding Time* (page 14)

Weather squares for use with *God's Weather Days* (page 19) and *God's Weather Days Graph* (page 19)

For use with *All Day Long Big Book* (page 26)

Place
child's photo
here.

_____
(child's name)

wore

_____
(his or her)

_____ _____
(color/description)   (item)

All Day Long!

Noah's Ark